Free Soul

Reflections

Selected Wisdoms
from Fifteen Years of Teaching
by Free Soul Founder

Pete A. Sanders Jr.

Compiled by Kathy Rose

Free Soul Publishing
P.O. Box 1762
Sedona, Arizona 86339

*This book is dedicated to
the Universal Spirit of Inspiration that
reaches out for and flows through
each of us.*

Index of Topics

Index of Topics

About the Author & Free Soul

Pete Sanders is an honors graduate of Massachusetts Institute of Technology where his studies focused on Bio-Medical Chemistry and Brain Science. Accepted to attend Harvard Medical School, he chose instead to pursue independent spiritual and mind/body research.

In 1980 in Sedona, Arizona he founded Free Soul, a Non-Profit Tax Exempt 501(c)(3) Public Education Program designed to teach techniques that help people learn skills for becoming their own best spiritual teachers. Free Soul has hundreds of instructors in the United States and overseas as well as an ongoing Instructor Training program.

Mr. Sanders' book *You Are Psychic!* (available in all bookstores) covers his scientific discoveries for "on command" ESP, mind/body healing, and exploring the Soul. It contains roughly one quarter of his comprehensive course.

The Dynamics of Being a Free Soul 10-Lesson Course has 80 techniques for Soul Exploration, Unlimited Potentials, Psychic Development, Self-Understanding, and Programming Elimination. It is available from Free Soul instructors or (through Free Soul) on cassette tape or as a textbook.

Also available are Mr. Sanders' books and tapes on Sedona's Vortexes (and how to find vortexes wherever you travel) and Advanced Workshop Tapes on topics from Positive Past-Life Memory to Secrets for Spiritual Abundance.

This booklet contains key phrases and thoughts from such advanced workshops and retreats. While not the specific techniques featured in his books, these quotes can trigger your consciousness to deeper insight and provide understandings for how to better *live* your spirituality.

For information about Free Soul, instructors in your area, training materials, instructor training, or retreats in Sedona write to: Free Soul, P.O. Box 1762, Sedona, AZ 86339.

Also newly available is *Access Your Brain's Joy Center*, Mr. Sanders' latest discovery for how to trigger the brain's natural mood-elevation mechanisms in seconds.

Keys for Using Reflections

This booklet is designed to be more than just a resource of inspirational quotations. Its primary purpose is to be a catalyst for expanding your own wisdom. In particular to become a collection of your own insights.

Opposite each quotation is a full blank page. This space is provided for recording your personal reflections on the spiritual concept put forward by the quote (or whatever other thoughts it triggers in you). This option gives you the freedom to go beyond the words of any single quotation by individualizing it to your own truth and perspective.

Knowledge becomes wisdom when it is personally experienced. As important as a quote may be, it is insignificant compared to the value of self-generating your own learning.

We have specifically designed an attractive blank page, because it is your thoughts and progress that are truly worthy of framing. Each reflection you have is a jewel of self-channeled insight and deserves to be recorded in a place of honor.

Even more important than what you write, however, is the process of forming your own spiritual truths. If you never write a word, but the blank space nudges you to meditate briefly after reading a quotation, then it has done its job.

The 52 quotes (one for each week of the year) are ordered to coincide with key holidays and seasons (if you wish to go in sequence). Because holidays can slide between different weeks from year to year, their themes are reflected for two weeks around that holiday.

Please feel free to use *Free Soul Reflections* spontaneously or in any order you wish. Allowing the book to find its own page can be a method for letting your Soul and Guides share a key thought for your day, week, or a specific important time.

Most of all, enjoy *Free Soul Reflections* as a mirror of how much you already know. If a quotation is meaningful to you, then you already have some or all of that insight within you. With each page cherish yourself for having and expanding that wisdom.

You are a Soul
that has a body.

Learn to live
the unlimited potentials
that are your birthright
as that Free Soul.

Reflections

Life Purpose

The term "life purpose" is
too limiting. Instead, I choose
to believe in "life purposes."
To find yours ask, "What are your
personal themes for this life?"
Which of them are you
drawn to be working on?
Ask yourself what interests you,
what grabs your attention right
now? In education it's called
"seizing the teachable moment."
Spiritually you could call it
"seizing the evolvable moment."

Reflections

Discontent

Discontent is the Soul's
natural preventative
against stagnation.

Reflections

Life's Peaks and Valleys

Life goes in cycles. It's an ongoing series of peaks and valleys, with the valleys inevitably coming first.

Take control and rename the valleys — try calling them "pre-peaks." The valley is simply your pre-next-breakthrough.

Realize also that the peaks and valleys are ascending with each cycle. The current valley is lower than your last peak but is higher than your last valley.

4

Reflections

Relationships

Any relationship will be improved if you treat the other person as a friend. Friends give friends the benefit of the doubt.

Reflections

Somewhere in our evolution
we choose circumstances that
will let us learn how to love
even if we're not being loved.
When you look at hurtful
situations, avoid getting into
a "poor little me" victim
mentality. Put it behind you,
without denial or avoidance, by
putting it through you. Cherish
yourself and say, "Bravo for
the courage I had as a Soul
to learn from that situation!"

Reflections

Love, Channeling It

Learn how to channel love, not just give it. All too often we're giving without replenishing. If you're not pulling in love energy from the Universe, giving it may be draining your storage. This process of depletion often leads to: "I gave you my love, so you should give me yours." When you truly channel love, there's no expectation of receiving in return. After all, you got the energy first, before they did!

Reflections

The "*problems*" *in our lives are just the scenery. Planet Earth is a beautiful school we come to for learning and experience. The problems we face — relationship difficulties, career decisions, all the complexities — they're just the stage setting. When they become too important, and affect our state of mind, our happiness, our peacefulness, we have let the scenery win.*

Reflections

Yes, Buts . . . (& Shoulds)

All of life has "Yes, buts . . ."
Don't let the "buts" of the
world get you down!

Remember also,
don't "should" on yourself!

Reflections

Life, as an Adventure

*Make life an adventure.
Your chances of finding
solutions to problems are
slim-to-none when you make
it "work." When you're on an
adventure — when it's
learning, your aura is more
open to the creative forces
of the Universe.
Keep it fun!*

Reflections

Here's a common, and unfortunate, way spiritual people judge themselves: They believe that because they know about spiritual healing, they're supposed to be able to do it all the time. That's not true. Planet Earth is about learning. Sometimes with an illness or during a disease, what you learn in the process of trying to heal yourself is more valuable than the healing itself.

Reflections

When you experience a problem
in your life or encounter an
interesting complexity, try
considering it to be
"Guide 101" training.
Do you think you could be a
Guide to someone else if you
hadn't gone through it
first yourself?

Reflections

Spiritual Recharging (& Dual Goals)

We need to nourish ourselves spiritually as well as physically. Going within and connecting with yourself as a Soul — with your true being — is an essential spiritual nutrient. Determine how frequently you want and need this connection for optimal harmony.

Set your ideal goal and your minimum goal. Too often we just set the ideal goal and judge ourselves if we don't reach it.

Reflections

You are cherished, loved and
needed by the Universe!
Without you, a valuable
piece would be missing.
Learn to trigger this
feeling all during the day, letting
it radiate throughout your Soul.
Give yourself this daily
dose of Universal love.

Reflections

Past-life memory can be more than incompletions or traumas. One of the ways you can benefit from past-life experiences is to recall a mastery lifetime, one that gives you new insight for dealing with a current situation. You've had countless lifetimes where you mastered key principles, concepts or perceptions. These are positive memories that can provide strength and wisdom to your life now.

Reflections

*Mastery of life has a lot to
do with being in command
of your state of mind.*

Reflections

Be a spiritual pioneer.
Channel a totally new spiritual
technique whenever you need it.
The Universe holds an infinite
abundance of skills and
methods for us to tap.
Learn to knock on the
Universe's door and
expect it to open.

Reflections

People sometimes make a big mistake in understanding the purpose of Guides. Their primary focus is to help you learn and grow; that doesn't necessarily mean just getting things "right." Your Guides are not slaves to "rightness" — their concern is for your overall spiritual development.

Reflections

If you believe that children are old Souls in young bodies, it makes sense that a lot of their acting-out is a reaction to the frustrating limitations of their current physical state.
If a Soul remembers what it's like to be capable and fully independent, imagine how traumatic it is to be stuck in a body that has to wear diapers, falls down a lot and can't feed itself!

Reflections

One of the best ways to enhance your love of significant others is to remember to see their intrinsic value.

It's the spiritual equivalent of, "I may not like what you're doing, but I can still love who you are."

When you see others as Souls, it's much easier to fully love them.

Reflections

Creating Happiness

*Each day do something
to create your own
happiness!*

Reflections

Allow Yourself to Be Learning

Far too often we put undue
pressure on ourselves to
be able to do something
brand new right away.
You wouldn't do that to a
young child, would you?
Why do it to yourself?
You are a child of the Universe.
Allow yourself to be learning.

Reflections

People ask, "Why should I
communicate with my Guides?
Why not go straight to God?"
Blending with the Divine, I always
feel at peace and in harmony.
But often when I tune in for
specific information, it's on a
frequency so far beyond me that
I have trouble interpreting it.
Your Guides can serve as
interpreters. They channel
the information in terms
we can absorb.

Reflections

Frequently we are
attracted to those who push our
buttons to trigger Soul growth.
When people rub you the wrong way,
take a new perspective on the
situation. Try seeing that
the person isn't the problem,
but that the interaction is the
issue, the challenge to harmony.
If we understand our issues,
our relationships can be less
reactive and attacking.

Reflections

Love, Even When Not Loved

It's easy to be loving when
everyone's loving you.
Once a Soul has mastered how
to be loving when surrounded
by love, what do you think
comes next?
Loving yourself when you
are not surrounded by love.
I try to see the people
I feel the most unloved by
as my greatest opportunity
to go to that next level—
to be more like my Guides.

25

Reflections

If we tie our satisfaction level to only one possible answer, we limit how the Universe can send us solutions.

Reflections

Make life a quest, not a test.
If it's a test, you always lose.
You have all the tension
of worrying about the current
test, then the anxiety of waiting
nervously for the next one.
When life is a quest, it's equally
passionate, but it's an adventure.
It becomes an exploration
to stimulate the Soul
and not just constant
survival pressure.

Reflections

Sometimes as people get older and their bodies run down they can feel like a failure. Ask yourself this: "Do you want to be a body or do you want to be a Soul?" If you're a Soul, you don't make your worth dependent on what the body is doing. You do the best you can with it, but you value yourself, first and foremost, as a Soul.

Reflections

Self-Teaching

Always consider yourself part of the "teaching team" in anything you study. Take the credit for creating the opportunities that lead to your own breakthroughs. Don't give away your Soul's birthright by thinking the instructors are the only teachers.

Reflections

Put-ups

When you are self-critical
and slip into mental put-downs, try
immediately to give yourself
a "put-up" to neutralize
the acid in your aura.
Regular put-ups are one
of the most simple but powerful
ways to improve your physical,
mental and spiritual health.

Reflections

The best way to maximize
your openness to information
from your Guides is to truly
not care about whether
you get the "right" answer.
The minute you start worrying
about "Am I getting it right?"
you shut down.
Worry creates static that
interferes with the signal. When
communicating with Guides, go
into it with the relaxed attitude of
"Let's see what I get."

Reflections

*Make the process of finding
solutions to your problems
an adventure. If your
focus is just on the result —
having the answers — you enjoy
about five seconds of happiness.
Give yourself fulfillment
from the whole process.
Actually the real secret
is in knowing the questions.*

Reflections

Self-Teaching Traits

What are some of the qualities you'd want in a teacher? Patience, compassion, sense of humor, open-mindedness, caring, creativity, playfulness? What qualities don't you want? Intolerance, inflexibility, boring approach, judgmental attitude? Life is a school and you are your own best teacher. To enhance your Soul learning nurture your positive traits as a self-teacher.

Reflections

When exploring past-life memory, keep in mind your purpose for searching into your past lives. Without a purpose, you might as well go home and watch the History Channel on Cable T.V.
Seek to specifically learn.
That way you avoid merely drifting in your akashic encyclopedia.

Reflections

Look for ways to put more
joy into your activities.
We tend to make everything
"work." A good example is
when we say, I'm going to
make it work." What we
really mean is, "I'm going
to make it work out."
Use your creativity to
be "in joy" with whatever
you're doing.
Play at it.
Don't work at it.

Reflections

How Can This Serve Me?

In times of emotional chaos don't ask, "Why is this happening?" — with an emphasis on "What did I do wrong?" Try saying instead, "How can this serve me?" — realizing that the situation can be building material for your next breakthrough.

Reflections

Imagination

One of Einstein's most powerful quotations was: "Imagination is more important than knowledge." People frequently ask, "How do I know if I'm really psychically sensing, or if I'm just imagining it?" It doesn't matter. If the imagining gives you an insight that serves you, that's what is important.

Esteem Building

Giving yourself an esteem builder every day is vital. Most important, find an esteem-building mechanism that is not dependent on externals. Identify an intrinsic value within you on which to base your esteem. Cherish what it is that makes you a valuable, lovable and worthwhile human being — independent of external achievements or relationships.

Self-Counseling

How would you picture your perfect counselor? What would the setting be? How would this perfect counselor first reach out to you? What would be said? A first gesture? How would they help you feel welcome and ready to solve problems? Identifying your needs in a counseling style is important. When you're in crisis, this is the way you should treat yourself!

Reflections

Soul Bruises

Soul bruises occur when a
past-life event was so traumatic
that it created an incompletion.
Because this trauma could not
be fully integrated into wisdom,
a wound or gap is formed.
Sometimes that Soul bruise is
so deep that it needs to heal in
layers. That's why we tend to
attract people or circumstances
that bring up the same issue.
It helps you slowly heal the bruise.

Reflections

Spiritual people often judge themselves unfairly about health and healing.
One of the biggest and most destructive spiritual myths is that if you're truly in tune, you'll never get sick.
Try not to base your spirituality on whether you catch cold or have the flu.

Reflections

Truth

You can't teach truth.
Each person's truth is relative to
their unique frame of reference.
What you can teach are
techniques that help people
to find their own truth.
Strive always to be
exploring "truth finding,"
not just "truth knowing."

Reflections

When you're working with your Guides and you receive an unclear answer, don't ask, "What am I doing wrong?" Instead, ask, "What could be the reason for the unclear answer?" Sometimes the question isn't clear. Or perhaps it's not the right time to ask. Maybe too much information would hamper your figuring it out yourself. Learn from the unclarity.

Reflections

Learning to self-comfort is
essential for full freedom.
It guarantees that
comfort can be there
every time you need it.
Just ask, "What would comfort
me in this situation?" Then, "How
could I give this to myself?"

Reflections

New Learning

When it comes to Soul
learning, we are frequently
our own worst enemy.
We sometimes think we should
be able to master a new level of
growth the first time it presents
itself. If the next level you're
working on is really a big step —
a major breakthrough —
something brand new —
how capable are you
going to be at it
initially?

Reflections

Inner Child

Unfortunately, a lot of therapies exploring the inner child use the "victim" model instead of the "challenge" model. In the victim model, you're a survivor of abuse, but often still seen as damaged goods. In the challenge model, the emphasis is on feeling good about the challenges you overcame. Your strengths are not just in spite of what you went through, rather because of it. Cheer that victory!

Reflections

*If abundance is really a
state of mind, how abundant
you feel is directly related to
how frequently you take
the time to appreciate
your blessings.*

Reflections

Wants

As a Soul, our purpose isn't to acquire the million-dollar home or 200 pairs of shoes. The Soul seeks to experience the learning that comes from the pursuit of our wants. Frequently you can't fully get the "what" of a want, but you can always work on its "why." The "whys" deal with learning — with what the Soul is questing to master in that situation. Focus on the "whys" of your wants.

Reflections

We've all probably had mountaintop lifetimes, — maybe a life as a monk in Tibet or Peru, or as a Native American Shaman. Being in harmony on the mountaintop is easy. Doing it in the village of life is the real challenge. Now we are learning how to bring the mountaintop consciousness into the village. Appreciate what a mastery level lesson that is!

Reflections

Perfection

Remember, the object is not to be perfect — rather, to be perfecting.

Reflections

Learn to be there for yourself.
Most people have mastered how
to get through "crunch" times
when they have outside support.
The next level of evolution is
learning to handle the stresses
when you don't have those
support mechanisms.
It's harder initially, but you
end up with a very powerful
skill. You become emotionally
and spiritually self-sufficient.

Reflections

Freedom

Through all the lights
of the Universe, and in the
darkness of every corner,
I shine forth,
for I am there.
Through all the walls of the
world, and over all the
summits that bind us in,
I am hindered not,
for I am everywhere.

I AM FREE.

Reflections

About the Compiler

Kathy Rose is a Senior Free Soul Instructor and Counselor who has worked with Mr. Sanders since 1983. Over the years she has served as a member of Free Soul's Board of Directors, as a Retreat Copresenter, and as an Instructor and Counselor Trainer.

A gifted Psychic Astrologer in private practice, Ms. Rose is also a Reiki Master and the mother of two old Souls in young bodies.

To Kathy goes the lion's share of credit for this project coming to fruition. The concept for a book of quotes was her idea and she had the perseverance to wade through years of program tapes to make the initial selection of quotations for inclusion.

Many of the thoughts have helped Kathy to live her spirituality, despite the rigors of parenting and a full time career. She wanted others to have the same benefit of those inspirational reminders.